MEGATECH

Artificial

Robotics and machine evolution

Intelligence

David Jefferis

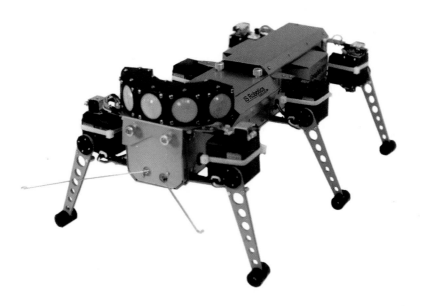

Crabtree

Introduction

I f you like computers, then artificial intelligence and robot research are probably the most exciting things you can read about. Machines that think are not just another idea from science-fiction, they are quickly becoming reality.

Artificial intelligence (AI) is already with us, at least in simple forms. Car makers now sell cars with computers that can understand the driving style of their owners. Modern airliners have computers that check the progress of a flight and help pilots control the aircraft.

In this book, you can take a look at the past, present, and future of AI and robotics. This is a fast-growing area of computing. Many changes are yet to come. In the future, thinking machines may improve the way people live.

MEGATECH

Crabtree Publishing Company

350 Fifth Avenue	360 York Road, RR4
Suite 3308	Niagara-on-the-Lake
New York	Ontario
NY 10118	L0S 1J0

Edited by
Norman Barrett

Coordinating editor
Ellen Rodger

Consulting editor
Virginia Mainprize

Technical consultants
Mat Irvine FBIS
Doug Millard, The Science Museum, London
Picture research by
David Pratt

Created and produced by
Alpha Communications in association with Firecrest Books Ltd.

©1999 Alpha Communications and
©1999 Firecrest Books Ltd.

Cataloging-in-Publication Data
Jefferis, David.
    Artificial intelligence: robotics and machine evolution / David Jefferis.
        p. cm. -- (Megatech)
    Includes index.
    Summary: An introduction to the past, present, and future of artificial intelligence and robotics; discussing early science fiction predictions, the dawn of AI, and today's use of robots in factories and space exploration.
    ISBN 0-7787-0046-1. (rlb)
    ISBN 0-7787-0056-9 (pbk.)
    1. Robotics--juvenile literature. 2. Artificial intelligence--Juvenile literature. [1. Robotics. 2. Robots. 3.

Artificial intelligence.] I. Title. II. Series.
TJ211.2.J44 1999
629.8'9263--dc21 LC 98-44481
CIP AC

Pictures on these pages, clockwise from far left:
1 Experimental robot.
2 1970s robot 'Shakey'.
3 Camcorder light sensor.
4 Closeup of a microchip casing.

Previous page shows:
Mini-robot 'Genghis' created by the US company IS Robotics.

Color separation by
Job Color, Italy
Printed in Belgium by
Casterman Printers

Contents

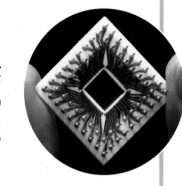

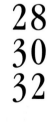

Robots and AI

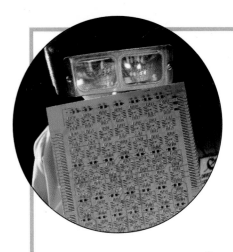

R esearch into thinking machines is moving ahead very quickly, but what actually is a robot? How intelligent can robots and computers be?

▲ *Toy robots such as 'Mr. Atomic' have been popular since the 1950s.*

▲ *Electronic 'chips' do all computer calculating.*

Surprisingly, there is no exact definition of a robot. The word itself comes from the Czech word robota, meaning 'work' or 'drudgery'. It was first used by Karel Capek in his 1920 play RUR (Rossum's Universal Robots), in which worker machines try to take over the world from their human bosses. Today, people use 'robot' for almost any machine designed to be clever. Robots do some of the actions of a human or animal, without constant attention.

R obots come in many shapes and sizes, but few look like the designs of science-fiction books and movies. For example, a robot welder has just one moving arm. A cruise missile is another kind of robot. It is shaped like a giant cigar with wings.

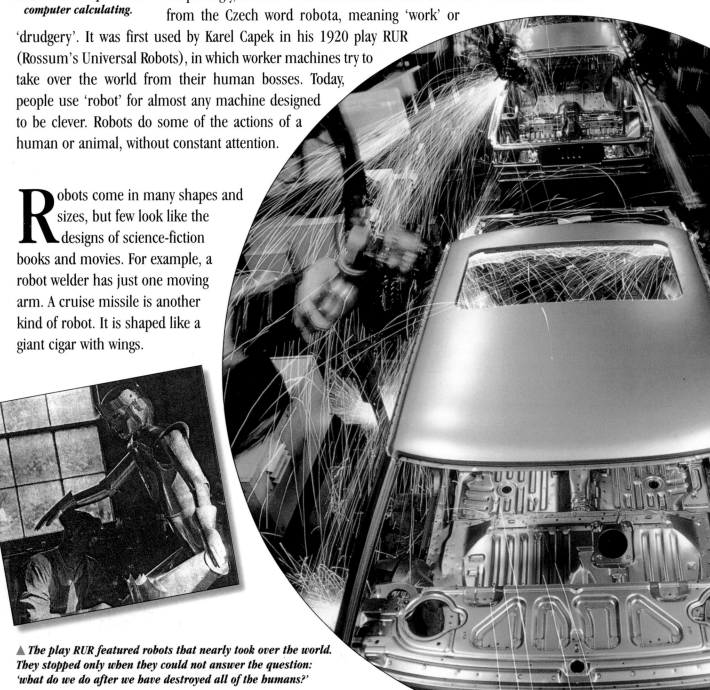

▲ *The play RUR featured robots that nearly took over the world. They stopped only when they could not answer the question: 'what do we do after we have destroyed all of the humans?'*

▶ *In Japan, research teams are working hard on robots of all kinds. Here a volleyball-playing robot shows off its skills. Note the machine's 'face'. It is designed to appear as friendly as possible!*

▶ *Astronaut Dave Bowman switches off HAL, an AI in charge of a spaceship in the 1968 movie '2001: A Space Odyssey.' Faulty programming caused HAL to kill most of the spaceship's crew.*

Artificial intelligence, or AI, is a fast-moving area of science. The ultimate purpose is to create computers that think. Scientists are working on machines that can look after themselves and make decisions that now have to be made by humans. Simple AI computers are already in all sorts of machines, from cameras to cars, and there are more to come.

Some experts believe that advanced artificial intelligence in the 21st century will think faster and better than human beings. An AI brain in charge of a machine body could turn the robots of science fiction into reality!

▲ *The next generation of space shuttles such as the U.S. VentureStar will be largely AI controlled, from take off and orbit to re-entry and landing.*

◀ *Car making went through a revolution in the early 1980s, when robot welders were brought into factories. Improvements included the precise assembly of cars and the neat finish of parts.*

▶ *This bomb-disposal robot is designed to operate as part of a team of machines, all in contact with each other, assigning jobs to each other as they go. Other bomb robots can go underwater to defuse or move mines that were laid in sand or mud.*

Caterpillar treads for moving on rough ground

Video 'eyes' at front

The dawn of AI

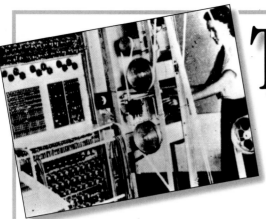

The science of artificial intelligence began with the development of early computers. The beginning of the computer age was in the 1940s.

▲ Colossus was a room-sized machine. It was slow by today's standards, but still much faster than working by hand.

Germany, Britain, and the United States all claim to have developed computers first. The German Z3 of 1941 was used for military aircraft design. The Colossus computer was developed by the British in 1944, during World War II. Colossus decoded enemy messages in a few hours instead of the many weeks it took humans. The U.S. computer ENIAC was the first to use 'binary code' in 1943. Binary code is the computer counting system still used today.

Early computers were big and unreliable. They used fragile metal-and-glass valves to control the flow of electricity in their circuits. Two inventions helped to develop smaller, faster, and more reliable computers. The transistor, a device with no moving parts, began to replace the much bigger valve in 1948. With integrated circuits, invented in 1959, thousands of electronic parts could be contained on a tiny square of silicon, called a microchip.

▲ AI pioneer Alan Turing. He came up with the 'Turing test', designed to tell the difference between human and artificial intelligence.

British mathematician Alan Turing was a pioneer of computer technology. In 1950, Turing predicted that by the end of the century machines would be able to think like humans do. For years, Turing's ideas seemed ahead of their time. Until the 1990s, even the most powerful computers were no more than fast adding machines. Today, many AI researchers claim that intelligent machines are just around the corner.

◄ An ancestor of the computer was the 1833 'Difference Engine' of Charles Babbage, professor of mathematics at Cambridge University, in England. His calculator was designed for the age of cogs and gears, not today's electronic world.

► *Glass-and-metal valves used to be a vital part of computers. They failed often and gave off a lot of heat. Today, such valves are a part of computer history.*

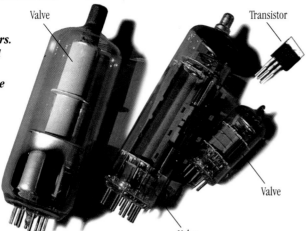

Valve

Transistor

Valve

Valve

What is artificial intelligence?

The term artificial intelligence was used in the 1960s by researcher Marvin Minsky, who described it as the science of making machines do things that would require intelligence if done by humans.

Minsky thought that AI machines could do things such as learning, recognizing patterns, translating languages, playing games, exploring on land and in water, and solving problems.

Minsky also said that intelligent machines should be able to size up a situation and choose a sensible action. If it turned out to be wrong, an AI machine could learn from its mistakes to try again in a different way.

▼ *Today's computers use integrated circuits, which place all calculating parts on a tiny chip of silicon. This magnified view shows (in red) about 500,000 parts arranged on a silicon chip less than a quarter-inch (6 mm) across. Imagine a huge city shrunk to the size of a fingernail. The city's streets would correspond to guides for electricity to flow in and out of tiny pieces of silicon, represented by buildings.*

The thick object that looks like a tree trunk is really a fine wire which joins the chip to a control panel. In the future, for increased speed, chips may use light beams instead of metal circuits.

Radio aerial links Shakey with bigger computer

Camera

Cables from camera to computer below

▲ *In 1968, the robot 'Shakey' was a leader in AI research. Shakey had wheels, cameras, collision detectors, and a computer. It also had a radio link to a more powerful computer which calculated the work for many of Shakey's jobs.*

Inside story

Today's computers pack millions of parts into a small space. The trend in computing is to put more speed and power into smaller and smaller packages.

▲ *Parts such as these could be found in a computer made in the 1960s. Today, the same parts can be made so small they are almost invisible.*

There are several reasons why manufacturers are making computers smaller and simpler. The smaller the computer, the shorter the distances signals need to travel inside it. This makes calculations quicker. The fewer parts a computer has, the less there is to go wrong. A computer with fewer parts is also cheaper to make.

Computer makers now use integrated circuits to bring together electronic components, or parts. Integrated circuits connect thousands, or even millions, of electronic components such as transistors and pack them into a tiny area. In an integrated circuit, parts are laid out in very thin layers on a slice, or 'chip', of silicon, about the size of a fingernail. It takes only one chip to operate a simple pocket calculator. A desktop personal computer, like those used in many schools, homes, and offices, may use dozens, or hundreds, of chips. These chips are connected with bigger parts such as keyboards and monitors.

▶ *Electronic components laid out on a printed circuit board, or PCB. Copper wires are printed on the board's back to connect everything together.*

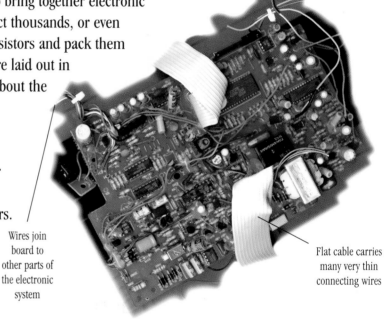

Wires join board to other parts of the electronic system

Flat cable carries many very thin connecting wires

Was the robot chess player a cheat?

Before the age of electronics, there were many robot-like gadgets, made mostly as mechanical toys to amaze and amuse. By the 1700s, some extremely complex devices had been created, including the robot chess player made by a German, Wolfgang von Kempelen, in 1769.

His clockwork machine, which won many games, shook its head and moved chess pieces on the board in a very convincing way. Von Kempelen admitted there was an trick involved, which was probably someone hidden in the robot's box, but no one ever proved it was a fake.

Computers will not do anything without a program, the set of instructions that allows a person to use a computer for a particular task. A math program may be easy to write, but creating a program that will allow a computer to recognize someone's face is much more difficult. Humans do many things by instinct, without thinking about them. No one has yet discovered quite how human minds work. This is one of the problems AI scientists are trying to solve.

Chip-making is carried out in a 'clean room', that is dust and static free

◄ *A gloved hand holds a newly etched silicon disk containing about 150 chips. Special lighting in the close-up (left) makes the chips gleam in rainbow colors. The disk is cut into individual chips. They are checked carefully, and faulty ones are thrown away.*

Computer programs are written in binary code. The normal, everyday method for writing numbers is the decimal system, which counts in tens. The binary system uses combinations of 1 and 0 to represent all numbers. The first numbers in the binary system are 1, 10 (equivalent to 2), 11 (3), 100 (4), 101 (5) and so on. In computers, thousands of tiny electric circuits operate as switches. When a switch is on, it represents the binary digit 1. When off, it means 0. This makes computer calculations lightning-fast.

► *In the 1930s, science fiction was becoming popular, and robots were featured in many stories. Tales of runaway robots gave writer Isaac Asimov the idea to create the 'Three Laws of Robotics' in the 1940s. In Asimov's fictional stories, these laws stopped robots from harming humans. The laws were fiction, but Asimov predicted problems that might happen in the future.*

THE THREE LAWS OF ROBOTICS

1 A ROBOT MAY NOT INJURE A HUMAN BEING OR, THROUGH INACTION, ALLOW A HUMAN BEING TO COME TO HARM.

2 A ROBOT MUST OBEY THE ORDERS GIVEN TO IT BY HUMAN BEINGS, EXCEPT WHERE SUCH ORDERS WOULD CONFLICT WITH THE FIRST LAW.

3 A ROBOT MUST PROTECT ITS OWN EXISTENCE, AS LONG AS THIS DOES NOT CONFLICT WITH THE FIRST TWO LAWS.

(HANDBOOK OF ROBOTICS, 56TH EDITION, AD 2058)

Sensing the world

L ike humans, robots and AIs need to know what is going on around them. Machine senses, known as sensors, do the job. Many of these sensors are better detectors than human senses.

▲ *A video camera 'eye' has about a million light sensors, all on a chip about half an inch (12 mm) across.*

Three of the five human senses, vision, hearing, and touch, are also used in robotics. Video cameras are an example of robotic vision. They may be used as machine 'eyes', seeing in color or black-and-white. A video camera does not have to be fixed to a machine 'head' like people's eyes are fixed to their heads. Cameras may be placed where they are most convenient. They may be linked by cable, radio, or light beam to a central computer's 'brain' – its central processing unit (CPU).

Microphone plugs directly into computer

▲ *A microphone can be used to speak commands into a computer.*

▲ *A missile-eye view of a target ship. There is little detail, but it is enough to confirm that the target is dead-center.*

M icrophones are machine 'ears'. Like cameras, they may be placed where they are needed. Many computers can act on simple spoken commands, and can also 'speak' themselves through voice-synthesizers. Machines that do jobs such as moving, packing, or arranging things need a sense of touch. This sense of touch is achieved through contact switches. When a switch comes into contact with something, it closes and sends a signal to the computer. Special sensors, called strain gauges, can record the amount of pressure needed to grasp an object. With such sensors, a powerful mechanical hand can as easily lift a heavy steel beam as it can pick up a fragile egg without breaking it.

▲ *Future robot air and space vehicles will have built in sensors.*

Powerful computers are needed to identify smell or taste. 'Chemical-sniffers' have been developed to detect the faint fumes given off by explosives. They are used at big airports to check baggage for terrorist bombs. Tasting is harder to do. One tea company, however, claims to have built a robot more sensitive to differences in blends than human tea-tasters with years of experience.

▲ *Industrial robots have six 'degrees' of movement: up, down, left, right, twist, and turn.*

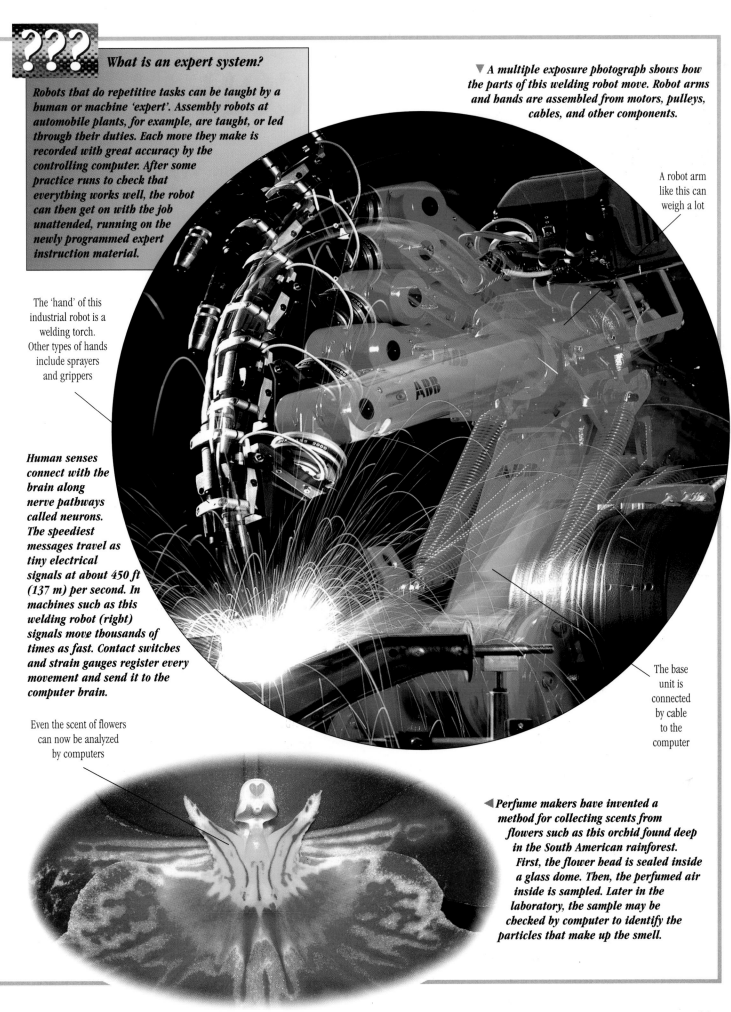

??? What is an expert system?

Robots that do repetitive tasks can be taught by a human or machine 'expert'. Assembly robots at automobile plants, for example, are taught, or led through their duties. Each move they make is recorded with great accuracy by the controlling computer. After some practice runs to check that everything works well, the robot can then get on with the job unattended, running on the newly programmed expert instruction material.

▼ *A multiple exposure photograph shows how the parts of this welding robot move. Robot arms and hands are assembled from motors, pulleys, cables, and other components.*

A robot arm like this can weigh a lot

The 'hand' of this industrial robot is a welding torch. Other types of hands include sprayers and grippers

Human senses connect with the brain along nerve pathways called neurons. The speediest messages travel as tiny electrical signals at about 450 ft (137 m) per second. In machines such as this welding robot (right) signals move thousands of times as fast. Contact switches and strain gauges register every movement and send it to the computer brain.

The base unit is connected by cable to the computer

Even the scent of flowers can now be analyzed by computers

◄ *Perfume makers have invented a method for collecting scents from flowers such as this orchid found deep in the South American rainforest. First, the flower head is sealed inside a glass dome. Then, the perfumed air inside is sampled. Later in the laboratory, the sample may be checked by computer to identify the particles that make up the smell.*

Silicon skies

▲ *A pilot's-eye view of an A320 flight deck. Sidestick controls are at the sides, while the front panel has video instrument displays.*

F lying an aircraft was once a big challenge for pilots, who had to deal with stormy skies and breakdowns. Today, computers in the airliner cockpit relieve crews of much of the strain during their flights.

A very simple type of AI was introduced to the airline industry in 1987, in the Airbus A320 twin-jet. The Airbus A320 was the first jet to use a fly-by-wire, or FBW, control system. With this system, electronic signals replace cables between the cockpit and the controls at the aircraft's wings and tail. Many aircraft now use the FBW system. A320s use five computers, which is more than is needed. The extra computer checks that the other ones are working correctly. The system acts as 'housekeeper' and gives the crew essential information needed to keep the jet flying right. The human pilot remains in charge and makes decisions during flight.

Wings hold fuel for nearly two days' flying

Inside the nose hump is an antenna to communicate with satellites in orbit overhead

▶ *The Global Hawk air vehicle is a big machine, with a 116.2 ft (35.4 m) wingspan. It has no pilot, and controllers sit far away in a mobile ground station. Their instructions are flashed to a satellite, which sends them on to the Global Hawk. It sends information back by the same route.*

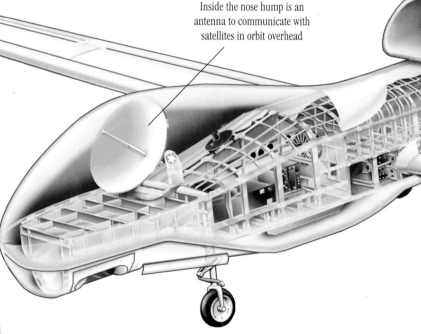

▲ *The 560-seat Airbus A3XX passenger jet is being designed with computer-aided flying controls, too. Its engines will also use a computer control system.*

T he main advantages of the fly-by-wire system are weight and safety. Wires weigh less than cables and are more reliable. Pilots training on A320 planes find something else, too. Replacing a traditional airliner's hand control is a fighter-style sidestick, which makes the flight deck much less cluttered. The A320 also does away with old-fashioned instruments. It gives the flight crew a color display system with six video screens.

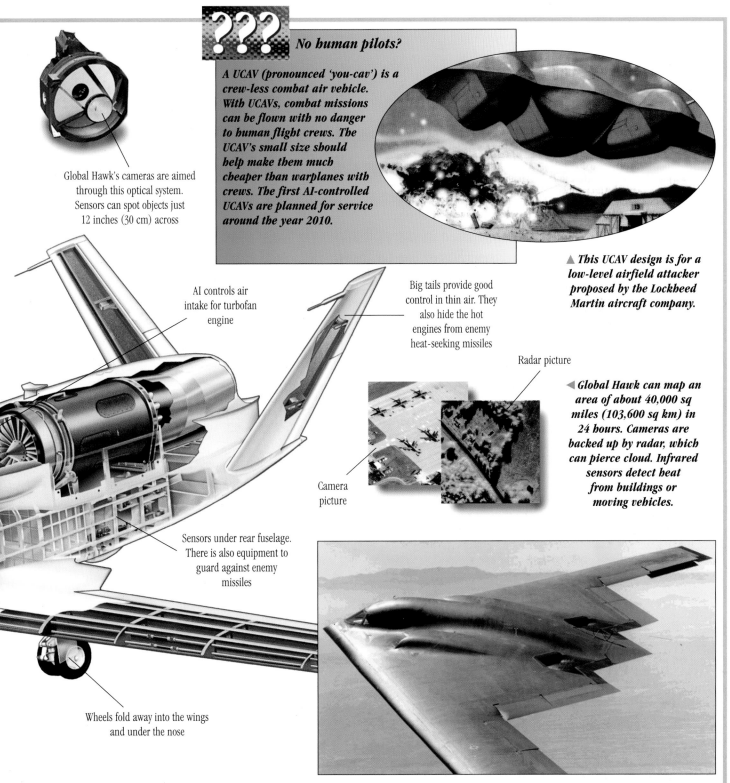

Global Hawk's cameras are aimed through this optical system. Sensors can spot objects just 12 inches (30 cm) across

??? No human pilots?

A UCAV (pronounced 'you-cav') is a crew-less combat air vehicle. With UCAVs, combat missions can be flown with no danger to human flight crews. The UCAV's small size should help make them much cheaper than warplanes with crews. The first AI-controlled UCAVs are planned for service around the year 2010.

▲ *This UCAV design is for a low-level airfield attacker proposed by the Lockheed Martin aircraft company.*

AI controls air intake for turbofan engine

Big tails provide good control in thin air. They also hide the hot engines from enemy heat-seeking missiles

Radar picture

◄ *Global Hawk can map an area of about 40,000 sq miles (103,600 sq km) in 24 hours. Cameras are backed up by radar, which can pierce cloud. Infrared sensors detect heat from buildings or moving vehicles.*

Camera picture

Sensors under rear fuselage. There is also equipment to guard against enemy missiles

Wheels fold away into the wings and under the nose

Crew-less aircraft, such as the Global Hawk, make great use of AI. Global Hawk is a 'sky-spy'. It can fly 65,000 ft (20,000 m) above a target for 22 hours at a time, recording events below like a sharp-eyed predator. On the ground, human controllers use video screens to see what is happening.

▲ *The flying-wing B-2 Spirit could be among the last bombers with human crews on board. It has a 'stealth' design which makes it nearly invisible to enemy radar detectors.*

In the future, dangerous attack missions will be flown by crew-less air vehicles. Bombers of today, such as the B-2 Spirit and Panavia Tornado, are probably among the last to have human crews on board.

Robot explorers

▲ Equipped with cameras for inspection, this bomb disposal robot works as a team with other machines.

Robots can be used in places that are too dangerous or too far away for humans to approach.

Robots are ideal for dealing with radioactive materials. Other uses for robots include deep-sea missions, bomb disposal, or even going into volcanoes. Artificial intelligence will allow them to work on their own in the future.

Crane

Camera with floodlight

Arm joints protected by flexible hoses

◄ 'MOBOT' was a 1970s machine that had grippers, cameras, and a crane. It was designed to handle dangerous materials, such as radioactive waste. MOBOT had remote viewing screens. Off site operators moved the robot's hand grippers by remote control.

▼ This mining robot goes to the bottom of the Atlantic Ocean. It sucks diamond-bearing rocks off the sea bed.

Space is an ideal place for using robots because humans cannot endure interplanetary missions that last for years. The Apollo missions of the 1960s and early 1970s brought people to the Moon, but robots have gone further in space. Robot spacecraft have explored much of the Solar System.

'Fly-by' probes have photographed all the planets except distant Pluto. Landers have gone to the Moon, Mars, and Venus. The Galileo probe parachuted into the clouds of Jupiter in 1996. In 2004, the Cassini probe will look at Saturn's largest moon, Titan.

Is space dangerous for robots?

The answer is a definite yes. Unless protected during a long flight in space, computer chips can be 'fried' by deadly radiation. Overheating from sunlight can 'cook' parts. Intense cold can result in cracked parts and dead batteries.

There are many dangers on other planets. The longest a probe has survived on the surface of the oven-hot planet Venus is less than an hour! On Mars, the Sojourner rover, launched in 1997, lasted several weeks, but its solar panels were gradually covered by Mars dust. In the end, the dust-covered solar panels could no longer generate enough power to recharge the machine's batteries.

◀ *In 2004, the Huygens lander will leave its Cassini carrier probe. It will drop into the murky atmosphere of Titan, moon of Saturn. Landing will be fairly slow, under a set of big parachutes.*

The Huygens probe is carried in a mushroom-shaped 'aeroshell'. This case will protect it during entry into Titan's atmosphere

The instruments will leave the aeroshell and drop slowly under big parachutes

O n space missions to distant planets, a probe with AI has a better chance of survival than one without, because there can be a long time-delay in communications with Earth. Even traveling at 186,000 miles per second (300,000 km/sec) radio waves may take many hours to reach a probe exploring a far planet. Disaster could strike before a command could be sent from controllers, who are back on Earth.

Future robots designed to search other planets will have to be able to look after themselves in case of trouble. For example, if there is an unexpected rock in the way, a rover cruising the deserts of Mars should have enough AI to be able to tell when it is a sensible choice to back off and drive around the obstacle.

▲ *How the Cassini probe might look as it passes the rings of Saturn. The probe was named after an Italian astronomer, Giovanni Cassini, who studied the rings in the 1600s.*

Player of games

Chess computers are not new. This early-1980s model used a household TV to display simple graphics. Even so, you had to be an ace player to beat the program.

Early game machines had simple graphics. For this game, color was provided by a tinted plastic sheet that was stuck on to the black-and-white TV screen!

The chess-playing supercomputer 'Deep Blue' calculated about 400 million positions every second as it worked out moves to beat human Grand Master Gary Kasparov in 1997.

Deep Blue's speed is almost unbelievable. It is surprising that Kasparov had any chance at all, considering that he probably calculated only about four chess positions a second. Along with other Grand Masters, he relied on experience and intuition to avoid having to think about vast numbers of pointless moves.

In AI terms, despite winning matches, Deep Blue was really just a super-fast calculator. For its maker, IBM, Deep Blue was a great advertisement and helped to sell similar machines. The Japanese Riken drug research laboratory bought a similar computer from IBM. The computer, called 'MD-Grape II' is quicker than a human being. The company claimed that a trained scientist could do what MD-Grape II does, but it would take a lifetime to figure out the calculations.

Computer games do not stop at chess playing. Users of personal computers and video games enjoy challenges such as space battles, flight simulators, fantasy adventures, and many others.

Robocup is a game with teams competing from around the world. It is a real test of robot construction and programming.

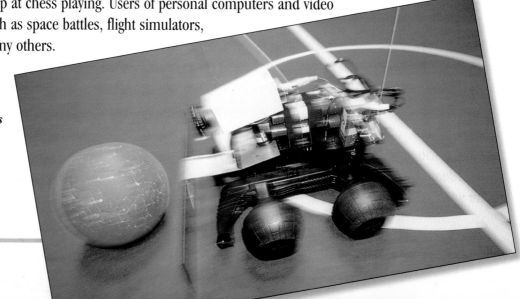

▲ *IBM's 'Deep Blue' was one of a series of chess computers, designed to take on human Grand Masters chess champions at their own game.*

▶ *Robot Wars is a TV combat game that sends radio-controlled machines to fight each other. Saws and drills are among the weapons allowed.*

◀ *One of Deep Blue's programmers thinks about a chess-winning move. Grand Master Gary Kasparov won the first game in the 1997 contest. Later results gave Deep Blue and its programmers the edge, and Kasparov lost the series.*

Aircraft images are projected on a screen outside the cockpit

Robocup soccer calls for team tactics from robot players. The robots must use their own programs together with radio information from other robot players in the team to chase the ball and score goals. They use similar tactics for defense. Robots play in different categories. The smallest category is for robots less than 1.5 in (38 mm) in diameter!

The robo-player creators are programmers who are fans of AI. Among them are space scientists who have worked on exploration missions to other planets. The scientists plan to send teams of small robots to Mars. The robots could help each other when a problem occurs.

▲ *Flight simulators, such as this unit from the Boeing company, are used for training pilots. Simpler versions are popular as home computer games.*

Robocup micro-players, with soccer balls

Learning by layers

A ustralian robot scientist Rodney Brooks likes to build 'cool' things. What could be cooler than the great science-fiction dream of a robot that acts like a human?

▲ Rodney Brooks is a robot scientist, or roboticist. He has made many robots for business and industry.

One of Brooks' robots is called 'Cog', after the Latin word cogito meaning 'I think'. Cog does not look much like a sci-fi robot. Cog is a screwed-together collection of wires, tubes, nuts, and bolts. It does have some things, such as eyes and a body, in roughly the same positions as humans.

Cog is very different from robots of the past. AI researchers in the 1960s and 1970s made machines that, when moving across an obstacle-filled room, were programmed to think first, moving only after they had worked out what was blocking their way. These machines could spend hours before making a move in the right direction. Brooks tried another idea.

▲ The mini-robot Genghis had six metal legs, so it would not fall over.

B efore Cog, Brooks made a series of small robots that had no reasoning powers at all. Instead, they were given 'layers' of simple instructions. One of the robots was called 'Genghis' (above), and its main instruction was simply to chase anything that moved.

If an object got in the way, Genghis went down one instruction-layer to obey a rule saying 'step over' the obstacle. If it was too big to step over, Genghis went down a further layer to 'back off and walk around' the object. In this way, Genghis and other robots scuttled around obstacles without having to 'think' at all.

▲ A slinky toy tests robot reflexes.

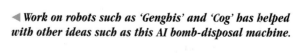

◄ Work on robots such as 'Genghis' and 'Cog' has helped with other ideas such as this AI bomb-disposal machine.

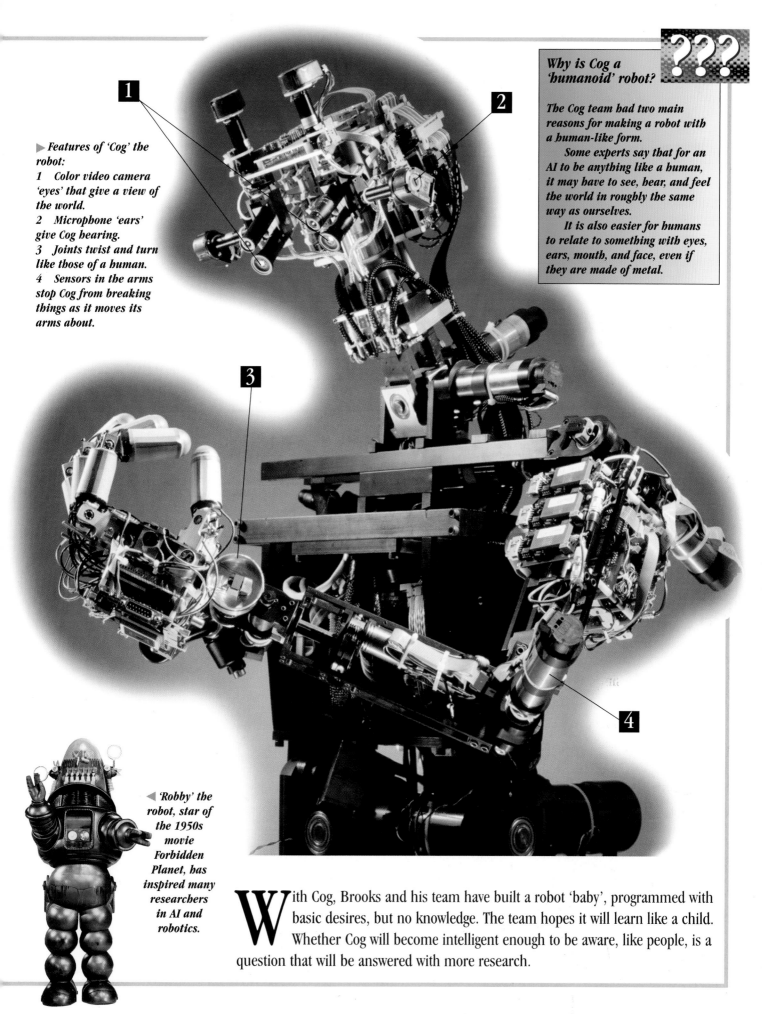

▶ Features of 'Cog' the robot:

1 Color video camera 'eyes' that give a view of the world.

2 Microphone 'ears' give Cog hearing.

3 Joints twist and turn like those of a human.

4 Sensors in the arms stop Cog from breaking things as it moves its arms about.

Why is Cog a 'humanoid' robot?

The Cog team had two main reasons for making a robot with a human-like form.

Some experts say that for an AI to be anything like a human, it may have to see, hear, and feel the world in roughly the same way as ourselves.

It is also easier for humans to relate to something with eyes, ears, mouth, and face, even if they are made of metal.

◀ 'Robby' the robot, star of the 1950s movie Forbidden Planet, has inspired many researchers in AI and robotics.

With Cog, Brooks and his team have built a robot 'baby', programmed with basic desires, but no knowledge. The team hopes it will learn like a child. Whether Cog will become intelligent enough to be aware, like people, is a question that will be answered with more research.

Neural networks

Artificial Intelligence researchers use neural (nerve) networks to reproduce in a machine some of the functions of a human brain.

▲ *One of the 'Seven Dwarfs'. These robots developed complex behavior from simple programs.*

A lot of AI research deals with the way human brains work. Inside the human skull, billions of tiny brain cells, called neurons, are packed together in an amazingly complex system. The neurons receive signals as electric pulses from all over the body. They process the information and act on it. Some instructions, such as breathing, are sent out unconsciously. Others are conscious, such as picking up a pen or turning a page of a book.

Even experts do not fully understand how the brain works. The neuron structure is too complex, and there seems to be no limit to the number of connections between cells.

Nature's original invention – neurons in the brain

Most AIs are no more intelligent than simple insects. Researchers are working on neural networks that 'evolve'. They believe that machine intelligence is in sight. Russian scientist Mikhail Korkin has developed a system that allows brain-like functions to evolve in seconds. Using this, scientists in Japan are developing a robotic 'kitten'.

▶ *A robot neural network has simple 'nodes' that correspond to brain cells in nature. The nodes make decisions based on trial and error.*

These networks learn as they go along, and complex behavior seems to come from simple programs.

Neural networks use something called 'fuzzy' reasoning. A fairly powerful system can recognize a dollar bill by being shown enough different bills to learn the common features.

Neural networks can also recognize

human faces, although they can make mistakes. A large boil, for example, might be mistaken for an eye!

Some cars are now made with 'fuzzy-logic', which is a software system that can learn a person's driving style.

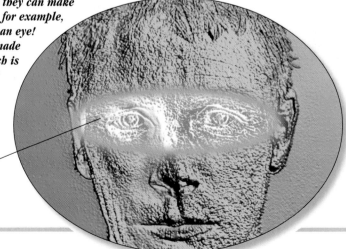

This program's purpose is to look for differences in eye structure

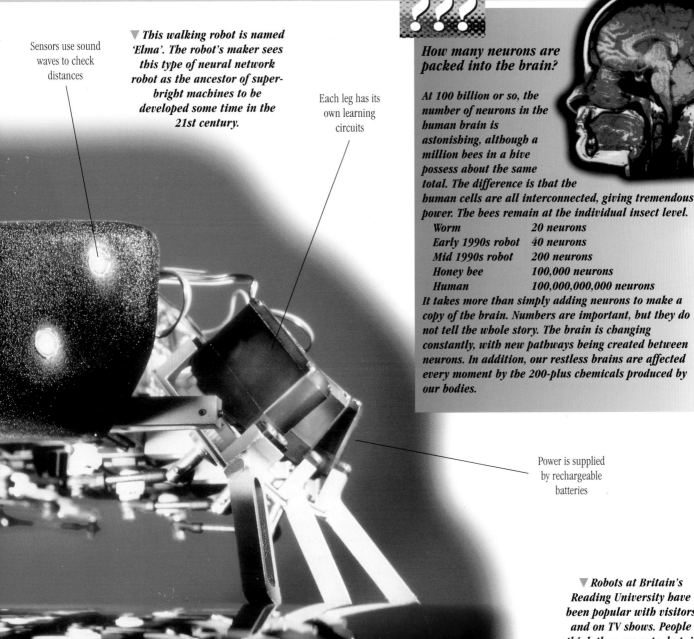

Sensors use sound waves to check distances

This walking robot is named 'Elma'. The robot's maker sees this type of neural network robot as the ancestor of super-bright machines to be developed some time in the 21st century.

Each leg has its own learning circuits

Power is supplied by rechargeable batteries

Robots at Britain's Reading University have been popular with visitors and on TV shows. People think they are cute, but, if the robots were bigger, their behavior might sometimes seem aggressive.

Another pioneering team is based at Britain's Reading University. Experiments with mini-robots named the 'Seven Dwarfs' have convinced the team to continue with AI research.

According to one of their experts, while the human brain might not change much in future, there may be no limits for AI. He suggested that, if you think of the human brain's reasoning power as the size of a house, artificial brains could eventually seem like skyscrapers.

Robot companions

T he idea of robots as friends or pets is almost as old as robots themselves. The difference now is that fiction is beginning to turn into reality.

▲ The K9 robot dog from the 1970s British TV show 'Doctor Who'.

One of the first robot companions was 'K9', the mechanical dog from the TV series Doctor Who. The robot was created in the 1970s as a special effects device, but the scriptwriters gave it a mind of its own, and K9 sometimes did not listen to its owner. In the 1990s, virtual pets, egg-shaped gadgets that were an all-in-one watch/game/pet, became popular with millions of people. Virtual pets showed that companions do not have to be flesh and blood, or even 'real', to be loved and cared for. This fact was not new. Back in the 1960s, the 'Pet Rock' was a passing craze.

◀ Virtual pets give their owners some of the pleasures of live animals. The Z-Pet eats, sleeps, plays, and goes to the toilet. Another virtual pet was named Tamagotchi, from the Japanese 'tamago', meaning 'egg', and 'watch' for its time function.

▶ Guidecane is a robot 'seeing-eye dog' that can help its owner safely through the outside world. Sensors detect traffic and other hazards. The owner feels movement directions as pressure on either side of the special hand control.

A nother techno-pet arrived as a spin-off from some U.S.-Japanese AI research. Half-bird, half-dolphin, 'Fin Fin' is a computer creation that exists only on the screen. At the time it was created, Fin Fin's maker claimed it was more advanced than a virtual pet.

Fin Fin's AI program lets it respond to the human voice, even to sulk and hide, and generally be more interesting than a goldfish or a budgie. Programs such as Fin Fin will have practical uses in the near future. Advanced versions are planned for running home services, such as central heating or even checking food stocks for supermarket orders.

◀ Fin Fin is based on 'artificial life' principles. It is designed to be interactive, helpful, and 'friendly'. Setting up these programs with a personal computer at home might allow an AI to do some household chores.

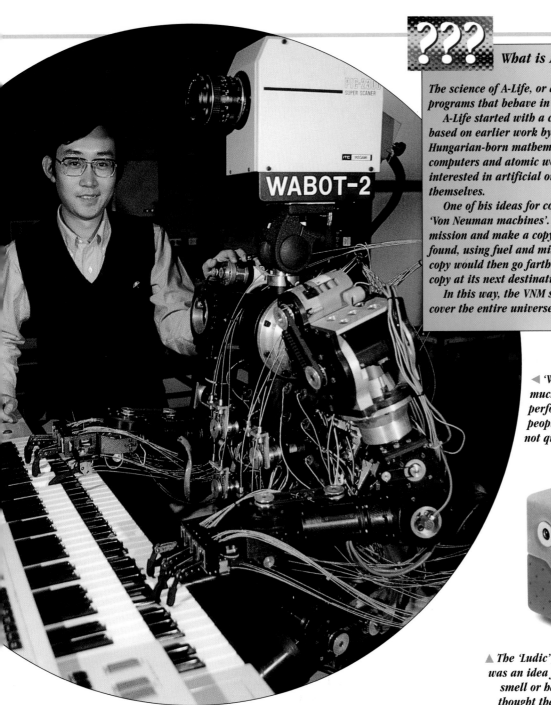

What is A-Life?

◄ *'WABOT-2' does not look much like a top pianist, but its performance is good enough for people to enjoy, even though it is not quite at award-winning level.*

▲ *The 'Ludic' from the Dutch Philips company was an idea for a household pet that did not smell or have bad habits. The designers thought that if it looked cuddly, it would be more attractive to humans.*

Programs that copy the human qualities of 'kindness' and 'friendliness' are planned for future robots. Researchers want robots to be able to do such things as caring for the sick and elderly. Japanese engineer Ichiro Kato has designed a robot that is a piano-player. The robot, called 'WABOT-2', has given many performances. Kato and his team have now begun to tackle 'Project Humanoid'. With Project Humanoid, they hope to build a robot that combines the technical skills of a thinking machine with human emotions such as kindness.

▼ *Sony's 'robo-dog' is a sleek 1990s version of the original K9 idea.*

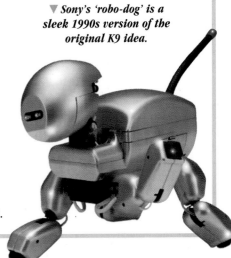

Project Humanoid is important because by 2025, a quarter of Japan's people will be over 65, and there will not be enough human nurses to care for those who are sick. If Kato's ideas are successful, these people will be looked after by robo-carers.

Cyborgs in sight

▲ *In future, human brains and computers may be joined together.*

The cyborg is a mixture of human and machine, half-way between a living thing and a robot. True cyborgs do not exist yet but the idea is not new – people have been trying to improve on nature's original designs for centuries.

A human/machine mixture sounds scary, but there might be some real advantages. A direct brain-to-computer link might let you store memories, so you will never forget anything. You might however, want to delete a few nasty nightmares! Being connected is already a way of life for users of mobile telephones and the Internet. With brain implants, permanent connection to worldwide electronic communications may be just around the corner.

The word 'cyborg' was invented in the 1950s, and is short for cybernetic organism, a mixture of robot and biology.

Super-senses, for better touch, sight, or sound, could be provided by add-on sensors. Super-strength may call for a mechanical body.

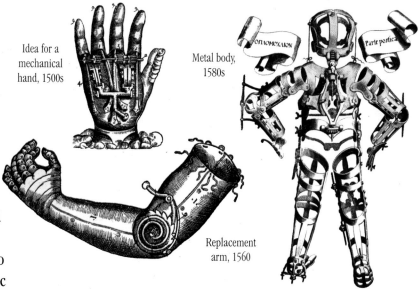

Idea for a mechanical hand, 1500s

Metal body, 1580s

Replacement arm, 1560

▲ *The metal hand and arm were designed in the 1500s to replace missing limbs. The armor-like metal outer body, or exoskeleton, was sketched in the 1580s by an Italian, Heironymus Aquapendente.*

Can the brain be linked to a computer?

Experiments by a research team at Germany's Max Plancke Institute have shown that joining living nerves to microchips is possible.

A rat's brain cell was fused onto a specially made microchip, known as a biochip. This allows signals to pass from the cell directly into the chip's metal circuits. Signals can return the other way, too.

It should be possible to do the same thing with human brain cells, allowing a whole range of possibilities. These could include:

★ *Electronic eyes for the blind, ears for the deaf*
★ *Using AI to combat brain damage*
★ *Brain link for electronic communications*
★ *Storing memories on computer disk*
★ *Boosting intelligence by linking brain to AI computer*

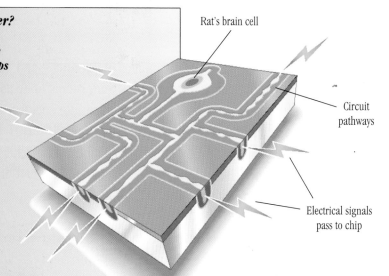

Rat's brain cell

Circuit pathways

Electrical signals pass to chip

◀ *Legs are often better than wheels in rough country. The 1970s General Electric walking truck was designed as a Jeep replacement. The driver made walking motions while at ease in a sling-seat. The truck's four legs moved in the same rhythm.*

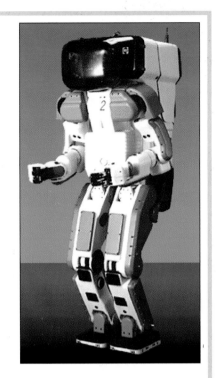

▶ *This 462 lb (210 kg) Honda robot called 'P2' dates from 1996. Using AI software for control, it could walk up and down stairs, and get up from a fall. Both were big advances for two-legged machines.*

Firefighter sits in heatproof cockpit area

F7   FIRE-AV

Powerful gripper for clearing burning rubble

Body and legs made from heatproof materials

Arm sprays anti-flame foam

A lot of research has gone into making a wearable outer body, or exoskeleton, for people who have lost the use of limbs. Artificial intelligence could bring exoskeletons a little closer to reality because things that seem simple to humans, such as balancing on two legs, require a great deal of computer power. Only the latest AI systems have this.

In 1996, the Japanese Honda company showed the P2 humanoid robot, a machine that could take stairs in its stride (see top photo).

◀ *A powered walking shell for stroke victims, made by researchers at the University of Wisconsin in 1976.*

◀ *Exoskeletons would be useful for missions such as fighting fires. A firefighter sitting behind the window could walk this machine into a raging inferno in safety. Biochip implants would link up this firefighter with AI at the fire station.*

What's next?

▲ *Electronic toys from Lego. The heart of this system is a microchip brick that can control all sorts of robots.*

Will robots become intelligent? Will these machines run the world? Will AIs get rid of human beings? On questions like these, opinions are divided.

Robotics and artificial intelligence have already changed the world in just half a century. It is unlikely that change is going to stop. Many experts think that artificial intelligence will soon go further than human intelligence, and some say this presents a threat.

There are good reasons to see danger, as AI research has very few regulations or controls. Machines may become more intelligent than people, but it does not mean that machines will push humanity into the garbage dump. Even in science fiction stories, there are good robots as well as bad ones.

◀ *This micro-robot, named 'Cleo', is designed to fit inside a human intestine. Cleo has a claw, and sensors to avoid obstacles. It can steer itself or be guided by a doctor using a joystick. Engineers are working on robots so tiny that if you sneeze they will blow away, like specks of dust.*

The idea of humans and AIs as partners, or humans with mechanical and computer implants, will soon be part of our lives. Real 'thinking' robots are also close to reality.

Japanese robot researcher Ichiro Kato plans to make robots that help humans and are kind as well as efficient. The robots in his 'Project Humanoid' would assist humans in a friendly manner. The idea behind this is that if a machine's behavior can be programmed, designers could make sure artificial intelligence reflects the good side of people.

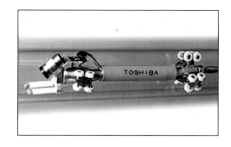
▲ *A useful answer to the problems of pipe maintenance – a 'robo-worm', one-fifth of an inch (5 mm) in diameter, that can scoot along inside the pipe, checking for cracks and blockages.*

Magnetic-drive engines suck in gases of alien atmosphere, squirting them backward for thrust. Engine pods swivel down for takeoff, hover, or landing

Antenna sends sights, sounds, and smells to humans back on Earth. Probe is AI-controlled but can take orders from base when needed

Planet is viewed with cameras, microphones, and other sensors. Extending arm takes small rock samples

Probe is about the same size and weight as a briefcase

▶ *Future planet explorers will be robots with advanced AI. This micro-flyer is designed for long missions, where light weight is important.*

O ne last question is whether an AI can be 'conscious', or 'aware' like humans. So far, no computer has shown real signs of this. However, as AIs develop, awareness might come gradually, as it seems to with humans. For scientists to know for sure, an AI might have to communicate on its own. It would have to say something independently, such as asking that its power be left on, when threatened with the 'off' switch.

◀ *A possible home helper in 2010 – an AI robo-butler, designed for help and service around the house.*

Three steps to danger?

For AI to pose a real threat to humanity, three major conditions must apply:
1. *Super-intelligent computers*
2. *Mobile robot systems*
3. *Communications linking them together*

All three are likely in the near future, and this is the main idea behind the Hollywood 'Terminator' movie series. In these action movies, the AIs of the future kill humans because they are imperfect.

Killer robots are always shown in the movies to be logical and orderly. They cannot 'care' for their environment because nature is imperfect. If, in reality, their intelligence allows them to understand imperfections, they too may want to protect biological systems like humans, and the natural world, instead of destroying them.

Time track

For thousands of years, inventors and scientists have been trying to make robot machines, yet artificial intelligence started only in the mid-1900s, with the beginning of the computer age.

▲ *U.S. inventor George Moore's steam man of 1893.*

2500BC Greek myths include stories of Hephaestus, the god of mechanical arts. He is said to have created the brass giant, Talos, to guard the island of Crete. Despite powers that include the ability to become red-hot, while at the same time crushing its victims, Talos had one weak spot – a flesh-and-blood right ankle.

1500BC Statue of Memnon, King of Ethiopia, blasts tuneful sounds at sunrise and sunset.

500BC Flying magpie made of wood and bamboo created by King-shu Tse in China.

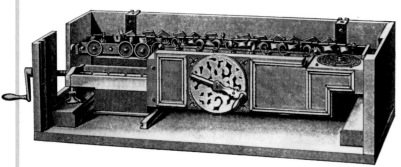

▲ *Calculating machine built by German mathematician Gottfried Wilhelm Leibnitz in 1671.*

206BC A mechanical puppet orchestra is made for the treasury of Chin Shih Huang in China.

1st century AD Greek engineer and mathematician Hero of Alexandria invents machines that include a steam-turbine and a temple-door opening device.

c1250 Albertus Magnus, a German engineer, makes a life-size automatic servant, which is supposed to be able to speak and open doors. It is eventually smashed to pieces by frightened villagers, who consider it to be a work of the devil.

c1235 French architect Villard d'Honnecourt sketches many ideas for robotic devices, including angels and human and animal figures.

c1500 Artist and inventor Leonardo da Vinci makes an automatic lion in honour of the French King Louis XII, to celebrate an official visit to the city of Milan in northern Italy.

1642 French mathematician Blaise Pascal makes a calculating machine.

c1650 Dutch physicist and astronomer Christiaan Huygens makes various automatic machines, including fountains, coaches, and music boxes.

1671 Gottfried Wilhelm Leibnitz makes a calculator that can multiply, add, divide, and extract square roots.

1738 French inventor Jacques Vaucanson makes a robot flute player.

1769 German inventor Baron von Kempelen makes a chess playing 'robot'. The machine wins many games, and the baron admits there is an illusion involved, but the secret is never revealed.

▶ *W. Grey Walter's electronic tortoises of 1948 could refuel on their own when power ran low.*

◀ *The Philadelphia doll, with a sample of its drawing ability.*

1800s Philadelphia doll writes in two languages and makes simple drawings.

1823 English mathematician Charles Babbage creates a mechanical 'Difference Engine' for calculating navigation, insurance, and astronomy tables. The machine was said to 'weave a pattern of numbers like a loom weaves wool.'

1830 An impressive 'speaking automaton' is shown in London. It is made by Joseph Faber of Vienna, who has taken 25 years to design and construct the realistic device.

1886 A punch-card system is used for the U.S. census. Its speed allows the job to be finished in 2.5 years.

Complex wires normally hidden inside a 'tortoise' casing

In the dark, a light tracks the tortoise on its way back to its hutch

► *By the early 1980s, automobile makers were adding robots to their assembly lines. Fiat was among the first European makers to do so. Here a car body is being put together.*

1893   George Moore's steam man walks at 9 mph (14.5 km/h), powered by a gas-fired boiler. Its exhaust pipe is disguised as a smoking cigar.

1930   In the U.S.A., engineer Vannevar Bush's Differential Analyzer is the first analog computer for solving differential equations.

1936   In Britain, Alan Turing has an idea for a machine for solving logic problems.

1938   The first machine to imitate the learning abilities of a living creature is devised.

1943   ENIAC (Electronic Numerical Integrator And Computer) is the first completely electronic computer, running under instructions from a digital program.

1948   In the U.S.A., researcher W. Grey Walter's electronic tortoises, 'Elmer' and 'Elsie', 'feed' on electricity. They find their way back to a hutch when 'hungry' for energy (see opposite page).

1948   First solid-state electronic device, the transistor, is developed at the U.S. Bell Telephone Laboratories.

1954   First magnetic-core memory, used in the Whirlwind computer, at Massachusetts Institute of Technology.

1956   Term 'artificial intelligence' is used for the first time, at Dartmouth College, New Hampshire, U.S.A.

1959   A laboratory to study artificial intelligence is started at Massachusetts Institute of Technology (MIT), by Marvin Minsky and John McCarthy.

1960   First industrial robots in use, controlled by electronic computers.

1960   First conference on bionics, short for biological electronics.

1968   First complete robot system is developed at Stanford Research Institute in California. It is a small, wheeled robot, called 'Shakey'.

1968   First large-scale integration chip, composed of thousands of transistors, is assembled on one chip.

1971   The first microcomputers come into general use.

1972   Unimation, Inc., is the first company to specialize in manufacturing industrial robots.

1977   First charge-coupled device (CCD) developed. Eventually used as a light sensor in many electronic devices, such as camcorders and digital cameras.

1980   U.S. industrial robot sales pass the $100 million-per-year mark.

1981   First IBM PC produced. With Microsoft software, the system eventually becomes the main standard for desktop computers the world over.

1984   Apple Macintosh computer uses a 'point-and-click' GUI (Graphical User Interface), designed to make computers easy to use. A similar approach is later introduced with great success as the Windows system, though the Apple Mac continues to dominate the graphics and publishing industries through the 1980s and 1990s.

1992   First compact disks arrive, able to store immense amounts of information on a shiny plastic disk.

1992   The Michelangelo computer virus attacks computer software programs around the world.

1993   Computers come to kids' movies with a digitally cleaned-up version of Disney's cartoon classic Snow White.

1996   Honda 'P2' robot can walk, climb up and down stairs, and keep itself upright if pushed off-balance.

1997   Sojourner robotic explorer roves around on the surface of Mars.

1997   It is estimated that there are 40 million transistors for every human being.

1997   AI researcher Hugo de Garis predicts 'artilects' – artificial intellects – for the 21st century, with superhuman intelligence. Neuron-count could be five times greater than the human brain.

2005   AI-controlled military aircraft coming into service; first automated cars and roads in service.

2010   New homes have built-in AI to run security, air conditioning, and general household services.

2015   AI-controlled spaceprobe flies to Europa, moon of Jupiter, to search for possible lifeforms hidden under the icy surface.

2025 and beyond   AIs achieve hyper-intelligence and self-conscious behavior.

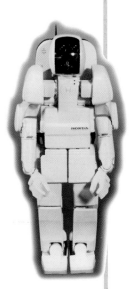

▲ *The Honda company continued to improve its humanoid robots with this 'P3' model of 1998.*

Glossary

A n explanation of technical terms and concepts.

AI
Artificial intelligence, a term used by computer scientist Marvin L. Minsky in the 1960s to describe machines that could perform jobs that would require intelligence if done by humans.

A-life
Artificial life, a science that studies life systems by trying to recreate biological processes artificially, as in a computer program. Where a biology student might dissect a flesh-and-blood frog to see how it works, an artificial-life student might create a computer-generated pond and frog to see how the two interact with each other and evolve. The science of A-life is based on work by a Hungarian mathematician, John von Neuman, who also came up with the idea of robot spacecraft that would move through space, landing

▼ One example of AI is voice recognition equipment. It is a fast-changing technology that is already more accurate than humans at identifying voices.

on alien planets as they explored further and further.

Android
A type of robot that is a realistic human copy, complete with artificial skin, hair, lips, and so on.

Binary code
Computer counting system that uses a series of zeros and ones to represent numbers and other information. Used by almost all computer systems today.

Biochip
Experimental microchip that combines a living cell with computer circuits.

Bionic
Living creature that has some form of artificial equipment built in, such as an electronic ear implant. Term was first used generally in a 1960s TV series, The Six Million Dollar Man, the star of which had artificially boosted senses and body.

Brain lobe
A term for one of the brain's two hemispheres which make up the cerebrum, or 'grey matter'. The cerebral cortex receives all your conscious body sensations and is responsible for learning, judgement, creativity, and some emotions. Different parts of the cortex are responsible for different functions, but the exact 'how and why' of the brain's higher functions are still not fully understood.

Carbon-based
A life form that uses the carbon atom for its structure is said to be carbon-based – like all life found on our planet.

Chip
Tiny sliver of silicon used as a base for the circuitry of a microprocessor device such as a computer; also known as a microchip for its minute size. Chips under development are so complex that they are equivalent to taking a road map of the entire world, and shrinking it onto a chip the size of your little fingernail.

Circuit
Any electronic linkage that joins two or more parts together.

CPU
Central processor unit. The part of a computer that performs calculations and controls other parts of the system.

Cybernetics
Name given to the field of robotic control and communications.

Cyborg
Animal-robotic crossbreed, combining a living creature with machine parts. Similar to bionics, but generally regarded as a more complete mixture of living and mechanical systems.

Evolution
Trial-and-error process by which life appears to have developed from organic molecules, through simple one-cell organisms and on to complex beings such as humans.

FBW
Fly-by-wire. Computer-run system now used in many aircraft, both civil and military. Advantages include light weight and reliability. Combat planes can use FBW to make complex and fast moves, giving them an advantage in air battles.

Hardware
General term describing any mechanical part of a computer system, such as the case, disk drive, keyboard, screen, and so on. See also Software.

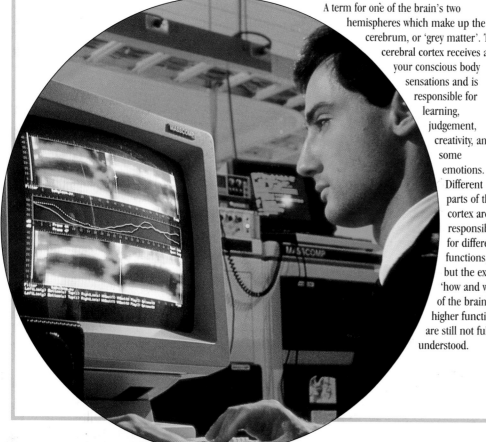

Humanoid
Having a form similar to that of a human being. It need not be an exact copy (see android), but should have a head, body, arms, and legs in roughly the right places.

Integrated circuit
A small chip of silicon that has many electronic parts laid out in miniature. Invented in 1959, the integrated circuit (IC) is at the heart of all of today's computing devices.

Internet
Electronic communication links between millions of computers across the world.

Light-sensing chip
The electronic 'eye' of a video camera, also used by more advanced robotic systems. It is a charge-coupled device, or CCD, that changes variations in light intensity to varying amounts of electricity. These signals are passed to the CPU for processing. The results can be displayed on a screen.

Mainframe
Ultra-powerful computer that can serve many terminals. The Cray computer shown at right is one of the fastest systems available. Such machines, with their huge processing capacities, are often nicknamed 'number-crunchers'.

Mono
Literally, one color. In practice, it is a term used in electronics to describe a black-and-white TV image, as opposed to the RGB (red-green-blue) mixture that is used for color television.

Neuron
Basic cell of the nervous system, which has the ability to carry and transmit electrical signals. A neuron consists of dendrites (branching projections), the cell body, and a long axon which carries the signal away to other neurons or to muscles and glands. Many neurons are packed into the brain and these are very small. Others, such as the neurons that run all the way from your toes to your spinal cord, may be as long as 4 ft (1.3 m).

Off-line
Term used to describe the situation when a computer system is disconnected from another system, such as the Internet.

Pacemaker
Machine, implanted into the body, to help a weak heart. It gives out a steady electrical beat, stimulating a heart to pump regularly.

Program
Set of instructions that is fed into a computer to make it work. A separate program is used for each major task required, whether that is something fairly simple, like word-processing, or more complex, such as CGI (Computer Generated Image) graphics that need to be created for a state-of-the-art Hollywood movie.

Sensor
General term to describe any mechanical device that performs a function similar to (or better than) our own senses. Cameras, microphones, strain gauges – all these and more are sensors.

Software
General term for any self-contained computer instruction program. See also Hardware.

Terminal
Any device, such as a keyboard and screen, that allows the input or output of data stored in a computer. A terminal may be near or far from the computer's CPU, depending on the type of system used.

Transistor
Tiny switching device used in electronic circuits. Has largely replaced valves (or 'tubes') which are fragile, bulky, and less reliable.

UCAV
Uninhabited combat air vehicle, pronounced 'you-cav', which is the shape of things to come in world air forces. Present plans include ideas for mini-bombers to replace conventional machines on dangerous missions. Traditional fighter planes may also be automated UCAVs.

▲ *This 1998 UCAV design resembles a mini B-2 bomber.*

Virtual Reality
In computing, used to describe programs that simulate, or copy, real life in some way. Using a Virtual Reality (VR) program, you can wear computer-linked equipment to see, hear, feel, and interact with a 'virtual world' created by a software program.

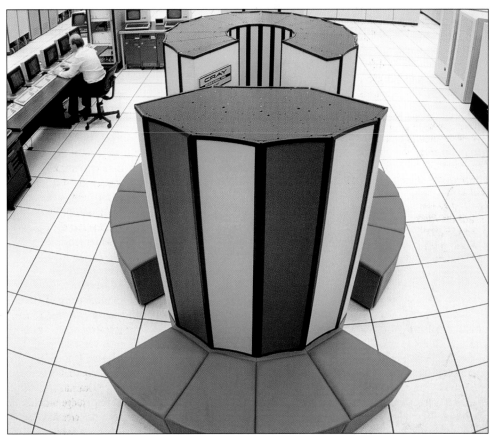

▲ *Mainframes such as these Cray computers are among the most powerful on Earth.*

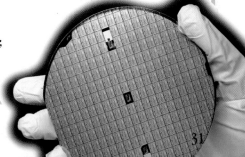

▶ *Silicon wafer, etched with dozens of microcircuits.*

Index

Acknowledgments
We wish to thank all those individuals and organizations who have helped create this publication.

Photographs were supplied by:
Airbus Industrie
Alpha Archive
The Boeing Company
Bruce Coleman Collection
Corbis UK Ltd
Dept of Cybernetics, Reading University
Fiat
Honda
IBM Corporation
IS Robotics
Jet Propulsion Laboratory
Lockheed Martin Corporation
Mat Irvine
Northrop Grumman Corporation
Sam Ogden Photography
Science Photo Library
NASA
Philips
Tandy Corporation
Toshiba

Digital art created by:
Tom Granberg/Renderbrandt
David Jefferis
Nick Witte-Vermeulen